THE
FATHER'S
Garden

RICHARD FELLOWS

WORDWYZE PUBLISHING

Cover Image: © ratpack223 | www.freepic.com

Cover Design: Bettina Kradolfer – www.bettinakradolfer.com

Co-Published by: WordWyze Publishing – wordwyze.nz
                                   Hamilton, New Zealand

Printed Softcover Edition: ISBN 978-0-6485883-5-1

Contents

Dedicated to

Kat and Daniel Wassenaar

Thank you for your friendship

and abundant love.

Introduction

Over the past two years, Covid19 has caused great concern in the earthly realms and a long drought in my own life of writing. Towards the end of 2021, I cried out to God for wisdom, direction and comfort. I started to think about the Father's Garden, the place of rest, and what was there. Then, one afternoon I felt revelation begin to flow, about how God's children are like "the sand of the sea" around His heartbeat.

I felt the flame on my heavenly pen come upon my earthly pen, and this book was conceived. When that flame comes, I can write for hours non-stop.

Have you ever wondered what is under the Father's throne? Hidden secretly inside the Mountain of the Lord are beautiful places to which the Bible alludes. Many have experienced and had the privilege of sharing their revelations with us here, who long for our Heavenly home. This book takes you on an exciting adventure to explore these areas.

> *"The Lord is My Shepherd; I shall not want; He leads me to lie down in green meadows. He leads me beside the still waters. He restores my soul. He leads me in paths of righteousness, for His name's sake." (Psalm 23:2-3)*

A meadow leads through a gate into the Father's Garden of Glory.

> *"The King has brought me into His chamber" (Song of Solomon 1:4)*

> *"Let my beloved come into his garden and eat its pleasant fruit" (Song of Solomon 4:16)*

What goes on in the Father's Garden? Some have seen a swing hanging from a tree there. We will explore its purpose and function. His Garden is filled with beautiful roses reflecting His nature – *"I am the rose of Sharon."* *(Song of Solomon 2:1)*

The Father's Garden has paths that lead to many seashores, one of which is the 'Ocean of Tears', another is the 'Ocean of Love', and many others.

Wendy Alec describes her Heavenly encounter with the sand,

> *"To My right was my heavenly Fathers rose garden... I would be sitting on the ground in this amazing meadow, singing like a toddler, happily playing, building sand castle palaces, blissfully unaware of anything else in my world."[1]*

If there are seashores, then there must be beaches, and if beaches, who visits them?

What else is under the throne?

What is the age of accountability? This question has puzzled many throughout history, and we will explore this and many other questions to learn about God's mercy, for God will have mercy on whom He has mercy and will have compassion on whom He chooses (Romans 9:15).

Come on a Journey to seek the beauty of the Father's heart as we go deeper into "The Father's Garden".

> *"The Lord God planted a garden eastward in Eden"* *(Genesis 2:8)*

---

[1] Wendy Alec; Visions From Heaven, Warboys Publishing, 2013, p.44.

God the
Father

The Father sits on His throne, clothed with the cloud of white mist. This cloud is the Spirit of Glory, Holy Spirit who covers the image of the Father. Around the throne and over the throne shines the seven rings of the colours of the rainbow. These rings of light are the seals of light of the full image of the Godhead.

The interaction and "forms" of the Godhead (Trinity) I have detailed intensively in my other two books (note in footnote)[2]. So here, I will not repeat that information but will say that God the Father is a person who has a form that can be seen sitting on a throne with blazing light around Him. Numerous scriptures declare this truth.

The Father has His very own garden!!!! If this is the case, then the Father can leave the throne to visit His Garden. If He walked in the garden with Adam and Eve, he is not permanently stuck on the throne. If He can step off the throne, then who is this Father? What is He like? Open any Systematic Theology book, and you are told that God is spirit; God has no parts. So who, or what, is walking? Who or what is getting off the throne? Our understanding of the Father has been misrepresented.

Norman Geisler, in his Systematic Theology, Volume Two, God, Creation, says,

> *Material beings are made of parts. Since God is immaterial, God cannot have any material parts. "Look at my hands and feet. It is I myself! Touch and see, a spirit does not have flesh and bones, as you see I have" (Luke 24:39)[3]*

[2] Richard Fellows, Heaven Through the Eyes of Children, 2021 - and - Granny Rainbow Shekinah, 2019.
[3] Norman Geisler, Systematic Theology, Volume Two, God, Creation, Bethany House Publishers, 2003, p.40

This statement talks about Jesus, but it can be used to talk about the Father. Of course, the eternal Father doesn't have earthly material flesh and bones, but that doesn't mean He can't have an eternal spiritual body that many have not seen. The Eternal God can manifest an eternal spiritual form.

God the Father also can move from His throne and appear anywhere in Heaven as a pillar of rainbow light. For, "He is clothed with glory and majesty" (Psalm 104:1)

The Father goes to His Garden for intimate reasons, work and rest; it is His dwelling space. He often just hovers off the ground, but He can also walk. One cannot see His face because of the Glory Pillar that emanates around Him and through Him, for they are all one (Trinity). But if the Father so wishes, various features of His "form" can appear through the shield of glory (The Pillar).

If the Father walks in His Garden, His *feet* must be active. His *feet* walked on the sapphire stone pavement (Exodus 24:10-23). Scripture tells us that the Father wrote the ten commandments on stone with His *finger* (Exodus 31:18) and that Moses saw His *hand* and *back* (Exodus 33:23).

In setting the scene of the Father in His Garden, we see that the Father can move from the throne, hover as a blazing Pillar of light, and move in His Garden and other areas of Eden. At times (His face hidden), He can merge His feet down and stretch His *arm*, *hand*, and *fingers*[4] through the Glory Pillar into a visible and even earthly realm.

A friend was told that the Father hovered and shimmered in the wind in Adam's garden with His feet unseen, but in this

---

[4] Job 40:9; Deuteronomy 11:2; Exodus 31:18; Daniel 5:5; Luke 11:20 and various others.

friend's Heavenly encounter, they saw Him walking in His Garden and could see His feet.

If the Father's glory were not so strong, we would see a full figure, an eternal One of the Godhead. Imagine what it would be like to walk with the Father and bathe in His love.

1 Timothy 1:7 says that God the King is eternal, immortal and invisible. Yes, invisible to those on earth, but His form is seen in Heaven. Still invisible from the blaze of Glory that shines around Him, but in certain places, He dims the light like a flashlight with different beams of light (High beam, softer beam). The Father can shine in various degrees of light and even reveal His form.

> *"The Ancient of Days was seated, His garment was white as snow, and the hair of his head was like pure wool. His throne was a fiery flame, its wheels a burning fire." (Daniel 7:9)*

Children
in the Sand

A 2nd century Rabbi, Yitzchak Vorker, spoke of going to Eden to look for a friend. He describes coming to a forest and then to a sea at the end of it. The forest entrance is a little down the Mountain of the Lord and is like a cave that leads under the throne to the Father's Garden. Out from the forest, one walks through the Father's Garden down to an Ocean, some call it a lake, but the Jews call it the "Ocean of Tears". This is where our tears are collected and stored (I cover this in great detail in my book, *Heaven through the Eyes of Children*).

> *Before Reb Yitzchak Vorker left this world, he promised his son that he would contact him from heaven and tell him how things were for him in Gan Eden. But four weeks passed, and his son didn't hear from him. He couldn't understand what was going on, so he went to his father's best friend, Reb Menachem Mendel of Kotsk, and said: "Rebbe, I'm so worried about my holy father. He promised to come back and speak to me, if only in a dream. But it's been four weeks, and I haven't heard anything from him. Do you think something could have happened to him in Heaven?"*

> *And the Kotzker answered. "The truth is that your father also promised me to come back and tell me what happened to him in the World Above. And I got worried when I didn't hear from him. So, I went up to Heaven to look for him.*

> *"Let me tell you what happened: I went everywhere in Heaven searching for your father. I went to the palaces of all the tzaddikim, all the holy people – of Rashi, the Rambam, Rabbi Akiva. I visited the place of the prophets, and even went to the very highest levels – to Moshe Rabbeinu and our holy fathers. Abraham, Isaac*

and Jacob. Everywhere I went, I said, 'I am looking for my friend, the exalted Reb Yitzchak Vorker. Have you seen him?' And they all told me, 'Yes, he was here. But he didn't stay. He went on....'

I didn't know what to do, where else to go. So finally, I asked the angels, 'Have you seen the holy Reb Yitzchak Vorker? Do you know where he went?' And this time I got an answer, the angels told me, 'If you keep going in this direction, you'll come to a thick dark forest. You must pass through it, and when the forest ends at a sea, that's where you'll find him.'

So, I kept walking through Heaven, and as the angels had said, I soon came to the darkest, most forbidding forest I had ever seen in my life. I wanted to run away. I started to hear a strange sound.

Finally, I came out of the trees, and found myself on the shore of the sea, an ocean so big I couldn't see the other side. And I realized that the sound I'd been hearing was coming from the waves. But it was not the sound that waves usually make... it was more like a wail, a moan, a scream – full of the most desperate pain. Never in my life had I heard waves crying and begging like this... And there at the edge of the ocean, I saw your father, the holy Vorker. He was leaning on his staff, staring at the sea. He never took his eyes off the water. I ran toward him, 'Reb Yitzchak, my holy friend, what is this place? What are you doing here?' He turned towards me, 'Ah, Mendel, don't you recognize this ocean?'

'No, what is it? What's that sound? What's going on here?'

'Mendel, let me tell you...this is the Ocean of Tears, the sea of Jewish tears. I want you to know that every tear is so precious to the Master of the World. God takes all the tears and places them here. And there were so many tears – that they formed this huge ocean... When I came here and heard the sound of the waves, the cry of all the suffering of so many, I can't tell you how much it broke my heart. And at that moment I made a sacred vow: "Master of the World, I swear to you by Your Holy Name that I will not move from this place until You have mercy on your people, until you turn all the pain to joy."

'My dear friend,' said the holy Rebbe, 'I will never leave this Ocean until God has wiped away all of the tears.'"[5]

(Lamed Vav, Tzlotana Barbara Midlo, 2004, p.369)

Vorker states,

"Finally, I came out of the forest and found myself on the shore of the sea, an ocean so big I couldn't see the other side."

If there is a seashore of the sea, then there must be beaches in Heaven. And yes, there are beaches in Heaven - Scripture hints on this. There is another beach (shore) on the other side of the ocean. On that side, the waves are not tears but the presence of God's love crashing into shore (ocean of love).

---

[5] Shlomo Carlebach, *Lamed Vav*, 2004, p.369 found on http://inourheartsproject.org/stories/the-ocean-of-tears/ accessed 17 January 2022

Scripture and Heaven encounters reveal that young children gather here and play, and the Father visits them.

> *"Your love, Oh Lord, reaches to the heavens, your faithfulness to the skies. Your righteousness is like the mighty mountain, your justice[6] like the great ocean. Oh Lord, you preserve man and beast... Therefore, the children of men put their trust under the shadow of your wings." (Psalms 36:5-7)*

> *"Yet the number of the children of Israel shall be as the sand of the sea, which cannot be measured or numbered. And it shall come to pass. In that place where it was said to them, you are not my people. There it shall be said to them, you are sons of the living God." (Hosea 1:10)*

Does the term "sand" just mean that there are uncountable people like the grains of sand on a beach, or is there more? I take the term "sand" to be speaking of the presence of physical people by the seashore, on the sand in Heaven. The same with stars. Scripture tells us that people can be like wandering stars (Jude 1:13) or righteous stars (Daniel 12:3 – glorified saints). People who are Believers (saints), shine in the spiritual realm (Heaven), as the stars do in the physical realm. In the first instance, "sand", is speaking of "like" something - children, while the second instance, it is a reality in Heaven - a place, a seashore.

In this book, I state that there are children on this beach, but adults are nearby (on another beach), showing that all descendants of all ages are included, but this chapter deals specifically with young children.

---

[6] Justice itself is a concept that stems from a love for community and care for the people around you.

The entrance to the Father's Garden under the throne is, as I have said, through a cave and forest, which comes out to a seashore. It is there where Jesus and the Father dwell in their Garden.

> *"So, the seashore will be pastures, with caves for shepherds and folds for flocks. And the coast will be for the remnant of the house of Judah. They will pasture on it. In the house of Ashkelon, they will lie down at evening, for the Lord their God will care for them and restore their fortunes." (Zephaniah 2:6-7)*

Often, in Scripture, a verse can also be talking about the Heavenly realms. On earth, as it is in Heaven!

> *"Therefore, from one man, and him as good as dead, were born as many as the stars of the sky in multitude - innumerable as the sand which is by the seashore." (Hebrews 11:12)*

We are told that many children will be there as the sand of the sea. Many have been rejected, but they will now be the sons and daughters of the living God (Hosea 1:10). They will pasture on it, and the Lord, their God, will care for them and restore their fortunes (Zephaniah 2:6-7)

It is interesting that "Pearls" are formed in salt water or among coral reefs.

Leslie Hardinge says in his book *Stones of Fire*,

> *"The Greek name for pearl is morganites, which is the form of the ancient Sanskrit Maracata that was taken at the time it was adopted by the Greeks. The Persian name is Merwerid, which is the nearest to the most*

ancient form Murwari interpreted as "a pearl" or "a child of light."[7]

Interestingly, pearls near the seashore speak of precious children of light. This seashore/beach under the throne is where children who have died in the womb, been wounded, or left earth before their time are cared for and restored to their fortunes/inheritance. It is here they get to grow and play with the Father. I'm sure adults are close by too, but it is the young children we are focusing on here.

Jesus' heart was always for little children,

> *"Then the little children were brought for him to place his hands on them and pray for them. But the disciples rebuked those who brought them. Jesus said, Let the little children come to me, and do not hinder them, for the kingdom of heaven belongs to such as these. When he placed his hands on them, he went on from there."* *(Matthew 19:13-15)*

Ronald Nash quotes Calvin on Matthew 19:14 that:

> *"Jesus bears witness that He wishes to receive children, and in the end, He both embraces them in His arms and blesses them by laying His hands on them. From this, we gather that His grace reaches to this age of life also... It would be too cruel to exclude that age from the grace of redemption... The children are renewed by God's Spirit according to the measure of their age until by degrees and its own time, this power hidden within them, increases and shines forth openly. It is an irreligious audacity to drive from Christ's fold those whom He nursed in His bosom, and to shut the*

---

[7] Leslie Hardinge; Stones of Fire, American Christian Ministries, Book Division, 2011, p. 271.

door on them as strangers when He did not wish to forbid them."[8]

Donna Rigney in her book, *The Glory of God Revealed*, reveals in her Heaven encounters this beach in the Father's Garden of Glory where all these young children are,

> *"The beach was like no other beach I had ever seen on earth, or on other visits to heaven... When I looked closely, with my eyes of faith opened wide, I saw that the beach sand was made of coarse gold dust... I asked Jesus why these children were here in the garden of Glory... These children are the offspring of the glory seekers on the earth. Their parents lost them, either in the womb or during their childhood. Death took them from them. They are enjoying the rich rewards their parents earned by seeking My Glory. Jesus explained, Daughter, I am a rewarder of those who diligently seek Me. Today I am showing you My Justice. On earth, children inherit what their parents leave them when they die. These children were taken before their time, from their parents. So, they lost their earthly inheritance. I am making sure they gain their heavenly inheritance that they will also someday enjoy with their parents, when they join them in My Kingdom. Encourage My children to diligently seek My Glory, My Will and My Presence because My rewards are astounding."*[9]

> *"His mercy extends to those who fear him, from generation to generation... He has helped his servant Israel, remembering to be merciful to Abraham and*

---

[8] Ronald Nash; When A Baby Dies, Answers to comfort grieving Parents, Zondervan Publishing House, 1999, p.67

[9] Donna Rigney, The Glory Of God Revealed.

His descendants forever, even as he said to our fathers." (Luke 1:50-54)

Rigney goes on to say that children can come up the path and sit on Jesus' and the Father's lap, and enjoy the Father's Swing in His Garden,

"I heard the sound of children laughing and talking, and even heard loud, childlike squeals of delight. A teenage boy was leading this group of little ones. He was guiding them from the beach to this heavenly visit to see the Father and Jesus... All were excited and eagerly followed his instructions to wait their turn to jump on the Father's and Jesus' lap. Even though some of these little ones were soaking wet from their swim in the ocean of love, they were still welcome to sit on their laps.[10] "

"Let the little children come to Me and do not hinder them; for of such is the Kingdom of heaven." (Matthew 19:14)

I have a friend, who I have often mentioned in my other books, who has also been taken to see this beach and seen these children. The Father walked with her "holding her hand" down a path to His Garden to see the children.

"What?" you say, "she held the Father's hand?" Yes!

"You are clothed with glory and majesty, who covers yourself with light as with a garment." (Psalm 104:1-2)

He is the eternal spirit, God the Father of all Glory. But out of His eternal spirit body and pillar, He put out His arm and

---

[10] Rigney

held my friend's hand, and they walked together in His Garden to the seashore to see the children playing.

> *"He stretched out the form of a hand, and took me by the lock of hair, and the spirit lifted me up between earth and heaven." (Ezekiel 8:3)*

> *"Your hands have made me and fashioned me." (Psalm 119:7)*

To reject Anthropomorphic images of God means Moses didn't see God's feet on a pavement of sapphire stone; God didn't give Moses tablets written by His finger; God had no face to hide when Moses asked to see it.

Ian Clayton has also encountered the beach in his heavenly encounters,

> *"I ended up, after a period, sitting down with Jesus on the beach edge of the shore, and He began to talk to me about the pain of my life and how I was not able to relate to Him because of the pain of my relationship with my brothers. What needed to happen was restoration in my own soul..."[11]*

The beach seems to be a place of restoration and healing by having rest with the Father or Jesus.

---

[11] Ian Clayton: Realms of the Kingdom, Volume One, Seraph Creative Publishing, 2014, p. 104

The
Father's
Swing

Under the throne, the Father has His own Garden that He walks in and has intimacy with people. Many report seeing a swing in this Garden, a golden rope swing (Hammock). In their Heaven encounters, they are allowed to swing on it.

Jewish tradition believes that the Song of Solomon is an allegory of the relationship between God and Israel. In the Father's Garden near His swing and Rose Garden is that place of perfect peace. Everything in His Garden is a reflection of Himself and the Trinity. His beauty is reflected in His roses – *"I am the rose of Sharon" (Song of Solomon 2:1)*. His swing is the centre of love, rest and peace.

> *"Awake, O North wind, And come, O South, blow upon my garden, that its spices may flow out. Let my beloved come to His garden and eat its pleasant fruits." (Song of Solomon 4:16)*

> *"My beloved has gone to His garden. To the beds of spices, to feed His flock in the gardens. And to gather lilies. I am my beloved, and my beloved is mine. He feeds His flock among the Lilies." (Song of Solomon 6:2-3)*

In Jewish thought, the Swing hanging from a tree is very sacred and almost forbidden if the tree, branches, or fruit are damaged. But if one is careful on the Sabbath, one can swing, a time for rest, reflection, and restoration on earth as it functions above.

Interestingly, the Tree must not be damaged. This is because the Father's garden is a place of healing. Those who sit on the *swing* reflect, rest, and are grafted into the Tree. They are being grafted, by yielding in rest, into the Tree and its branches, and it's producing fruit in them which will flow from them in time.

The symbol of being grafted in the tree as one swings (not saying this is the Tree of Life) is like our abiding in God. Proverbs 3:18 (NLT) says of Wisdom (the Holy Spirit), "Wisdom is a tree of life to those who embrace her; happy are those who hold her tightly." The Holy Spirit brings forth the fruit of the Spirit. (Galatians 5:22-25). We could say Jesus is the Tree of Life; because of Him, we grow spiritually and flourish, while the Father is the dresser/gardener (John 15).

Jewish teaching says,

"As long as the swing or hammock is indirectly attached to the tree before Shabbat, and using it doesn't cause any part of the tree to shake, it is permitted to make use of it on Shabbat." [12]

"If, however, no part of the tree will shake in the process of using the hammock, then from the letter of the law, it may be used." [13]

There is great importance pressed that the Tree or fruit are not damaged, telling spiritual truths.

Donna Rigney on Elijah List reveals that she has also seen the Father sitting on His Swing in Heaven,

" 'Stay hopeful and hope-filled, no matter how long it takes. Trust me to fulfil my promises to my prophets and to you' - I heard Jesus say to me, as we danced together in the garden of glory. Father sat on His Swing." [14]

---

[12] https://www.chabad.org/library/article_cdo/aid/4423167/jewish/Swing-or-Hammock-Attached-to-a-Tree-on-Shabbat.htm accessed 18/1/2022
[13] https://shulchanaruchharav.com/halacha/hammock-and-swing/ accessed 18/1/2022

[14] https://www.elijahlist.com/words/display_word.html?ID=26596 accessed

"Adonai your God is in your midst, a mighty Saviour. He will delight over you with joy. He will quiet you with His love. He will dance for joy over you with song." (Zephaniah 3:17 TLV)

To dance "over you" means to dance around you, to spin around, to dance together!

The Swing is a golden colour glowing with glory, which Holy Spirit overshadows with His presence bringing shade.

"Like an apple tree among the trees of the wood, so is my beloved among his fruit. I sat down in His shade with great delight. And His fruit was sweet to my taste." (Song of Solomon 2:3)

"Of the wood of Lebanon, Solomon the king made himself a Palanquin. He made its pillars of silver, his supports of Gold. Its seat of purple, its interior paved with Love." (Song of Solomon 3:9-10)

In many cultures, a Palanquin[15] is a swinging chair. There are different types: a chair carried on poles or a couch swinging on ropes, like a large hammock. Names given are 'cradle swing', 'sedan chair', or even 'love swing'. There are even poems[16] that speak of the palanquin as a love swing. A type of eloquent couch swing attached to a large branch in the garden is also portrayed.

A Palanquin is a Love Swing!!!!

18/1/2022

[15] See Bibliography for links.

[16] https://www.poetryloverspace.com/poets/stevenson/travel.html and https://creativereligious.com/palanquin-bearers-poem-by-sarojini-naidu/

As we yield to God in intimacy, His presence produces fruit in us, and we start to cultivate our own gardens in the fields of Heaven.

> *"Now he who plants and he who waters are one, and each one will receive his own reward according to his own labour. For we are God's fellow workers, you are God's field, you are God's building." (1 Corinthians 3:9)*

Many of us will never experience being in Father God's Garden (unless caught up) while living our time on earth. Still, in spirit, as we do things on earth and spend time with God, we may appear there without us knowing it, for we are seated in Heavenly places (Ephesians 2:6).

Wendy Alec also shows how the Father's Garden brings healing through resting with Him,

> *"But always to my right was the Father's own garden, and the Father Himself would be walking, sometimes standing quietly, just watching me protectively... I looked up towards My Heavenly Father in His garden. 'Daddy, what is happening?' 'Your wounds are wounds of a great battle, beloved. The glass that falls from your head is trauma. The more you play, the more you rest as a little child in My presence, and the more healing of your body and your mind takes place on earth... Beloved, many in My Church do not yet understand how to heal those that have been wounded in battle. That is why it is so important that every wounded warrior runs directly to Me. For in this present Church age, it is sometimes I, and I alone, who*

can bring the healing balm that is essential to heal the wounds of this present age. '"[17]

---

[17] Alec; Visions of Heaven, WarBoys Publishing, 2013, p. 45-46

Age of
Accountability

Throughout history, many have searched the Scriptures from concern and broken hearts, seeking to find an age of accountability. What do I mean by "age of accountability"? Is there an "age" in one's life when one has the capacity to understand the revelation of the saving light of God, at which one is accountable without excuse for one's actions? Are there some to whom God shows mercy and saves if they die before reaching that age? What happens to children who die in infancy or people with a mental disability, whose intellectual and moral judgment cannot surpass young children?

What happens to aborted babies or young ones (children) in Heathen nations who do not have the light of saving revelation?

From Scripture and a Calvinistic understanding, there are answers, but also Heaven has revealed that God's ways are deeper than ours, and we don't know the full understanding of the Scriptures (John Calvin got a lot right, but not all). I can tell you right now that what I'm about to share brings hope, but I emphasise that the doctrine/theory of Universalism is false (not all the world will be saved). Yet many are saved that we would have looked over or thought were impossible.

The Jews have always had an understanding of the concept of an "age of accountability":

> *"In Jewish tradition before the age of thirteen, the spiritual accountability for a male child to keep the Torah is said to belong to the parents, but after the age of thirteen, he is considered to be morally accountable to keep the commandments for himself. For a girl, the age of accountability is considered to be twelve" (Bar Mitzvah, New World Encyclopaedia)*

The idea is that under the age of twelve or thirteen, a person is not accountable for their actions. Their parent/carer is responsible for training them to reach that age of accountability. The Jews even understand that this age can shift depending on people's intellect. Scripture even points to an age of under twenty. Now, I'm not trying to prove the perfect age, but that the concept exists in Jewish thought.

> *"The carcasses of you who have complained against Me shall fall in this wilderness, all of you who were numbered, according to your entire number, from twenty years old and above. Except for Caleb, the son of Jephunneh and Joshua, the son of Nun, you shall by no means enter the land which I swore I would make you dwell in. But your little ones, whom you said would be victims, I will bring in, and they shall know the land which you have despised." (Numbers 14:29-31)*

According to the above Scripture, at least in this instance, God considered those under the age of twenty not responsible for the rebellion to the same extent as those twenty or older. Now, I'm not saying that twenty is the age of accountability for salvation, I'm saying that one can see the concept in Scripture of an "age of accountability."

The Church Father, Tertullian, mentions the age of accountability as the puberty of the soul.

> *"In pursuance of what aspect of the association of body and soul that we now have to consider, we maintain that the puberty of the soul coincides with that of the body. Generally speaking, they both attain together this full growth at about the fourteenth year of life. The soul attains it by the suggestion of the senses, and the body attains it by the growth of the bodily members. I do not mention the age of fourteen because reflection*

begins at that age. Nor do I choose it because civil laws date commencement of the real business of life from this age. Rather, I choose it because this was the appointed age from the very first." (Tertullian, 210 AD)

Stepping Stones in Revealing the Concept of an Age of Accountability

In revealing this concept, we will take stepping stones and lay its truth out step by step.

*   The Bible is clear that "We have all sinned and fallen short of the glory of God." (Romans 3:23)

*   Infants do not know good and evil (Deuteronomy 1:39). Infants lack the ability to perform good or morally evil acts. Jeremiah 19:4 says they are innocent in the context of not knowing.

*   All are born with a sinful nature. This damage means we are no longer clothed with God's glory as Adam was before he sinned.

*   David wrote, "Surely I was sinful at birth (that nature is waiting to manifest), sinful from the time my mother conceived me" (Psalms 51:5). Psalm 58:3 tells us, "Even from birth the wicked go astray, from the womb they are wayward and speak lies."

* People go astray, wayward because the seed of sin is there waiting to sprout, give birth. If people allow this sin to take root and grow and control their lives, they become wicked.

* All who are born have fallen and are in need of experiencing the glory of God to be saved, but because we will tend towards sinning as we grow, we cannot attain this glory by ourselves.

* So, without the atonement of Jesus and the sovereign regeneration of God - none can be saved. God provided a way to be saved because people are incapable of living glorious lives in God while living in a fallen existence because they have a sinful nature. But accountability and judgment are based on "knowingly doing immoral acts".

* Their sin nature needs to be saved, but the manifestation of that nature in moral conviction has not come forth yet in deeds until the age of accountability.

* Scripture tells us that for some, God marks them out before they are born and saves them in their mother's womb. That means God can save babies or anyone who has no functioning conscience. *"Before I formed you in the womb I knew you, before you were born, I set you apart; I appointed you as a prophet to the nations."* (Jeremiah 1:5). John the Baptist was even saved in his mother's womb because salvation is by God's Grace. *"He shall be filled with the Holy Spirit, even from his mother's womb."* (Luke 1:15).

* 1 Corinthians 5:10 says, *"For we must all appear before the judgement seat of Christ, that each one may receive what is due him for the things done while in the body, whether good or bad"* - Judgment deals with sins committed.

* Revelation 20:12-13 says, *"The dead were judged according to what they had done as recorded in the books. The sea gave up the dead that were in it, and death and hades gave up the dead that was in them, and each person was judged according to what he had done."*

R.A. Webb says,

"Dead infants have been prevented by the providence of God from committing any responsible deeds of any sort in the body, and consequently infants are not damnable upon these premises."[18]

Ronald Nash says,

"Adults who die in an unbelieving, unregenerate state have rejected the truth in general revelation (Romans 1) and have committed evil deeds in the body and hence judged justly."[19]

We have seen so far that God, by His Mercy, can save aborted babies, young infants, and the mentally challenged from His Justice. He gives the new birth and regeneration in moments of life here or as they are passing out of this life.

---

[18] R.A. Webb, *The Theology of Infant Salvation*, Richmond VA; PrebyterianCommittee of Publication, 1907 p. 42
[19] R. Nash, *When a Baby Dies; Answers to comfort grieving parents*, Zondervan Publishing, 1999 p.62

"For He says to Moses, I will have mercy on whomever I will have mercy, and will have compassion on whomever I will have compassion" (Romans 9:15)

But what about older children and people who have little revelation (Tribes, Heathen)? A Heaven revelation has revealed that an "age of accountability" to the light does exist, and this age can differ in different places. In saying this, it does not mean all adults will be saved, nor is it promoting Universalism.

Does God care about the Heathen?

Well, of course He does, for He sent His Son to die for the *world*. In my early Calvinistic, Reformed years, I used to think God was just focused on one special chosen people in the Old Testament (and that is partly true, but there is more). That He was saving a people out of a fallen world. These following Scriptures used to control my interpretation:

Dr. Robert Reymond,

"He left the Gentiles nations "alienated from citizenship in Israel and foreigners to the covenants of promise, without hope, and without God in the world (Ephesians 2:12). Throughout the Old Testament times, he "Let all nations go their own way (Acts 14:16) and "Overlooked their ignorance" in the sense that he did nothing to directly overcome it (Acts 17:30). Exclusively to Israel did God entrust the oracles of God (Romans 3:1-2). And the Psalmist even evokes praise to the Lord because, "He has revealed his word to Jacob, his laws and decrees to Israel. He has done this for no other nation, they do not know his laws (Psalms 147:19-20). Furthermore, God declared to Israel

through Amos, "You only have I known, of all the families of the earth" (Amos 3:2).[20]

These verses are pretty strong, but is there only one way to interpret them? It is true that God chose Israel out of all other nations to be a people set apart and left other nations in their ways. Israel was to be a blessing to other nations so that other nations would learn of the Living God through them, and when Christ came (Jesus), He brought salvation to *all* nations.

Does that mean those nations before Christ just miss out and are damned? No! There is revelation from Heaven of an age of accountability and judgment according to the measure of revelatory light. This does not mean all adults will be saved, as general revelation damns, but there are some by God's Grace, whom He saves out of the heathen, due to an age of accountability, and that age can differ in different cultures. Those that come out of heathen areas into Heaven by God's Grace have a special area in Paradise they go to grow in revelation and the ways of Christ. Over time, they will enter into the fold with the others who were blessed with a sovereign higher calling and purpose to know and grow in Christ on earth.

Israel and those who have come to Christ through the preaching of the Gospel were called with a sovereign higher calling in the earth to bring and shine the light. Although Israel as a nation was set apart, to keep them as a pure genealogy for Christ's entry into the world, not all Israelites will make it into Heaven. Once past the 'age of accountability', this side of the Cross, you still have to put your faith in Jesus Christ as the Messiah. But others, such as infants who die in the womb, young children, mentally challenged, and those young in heathen

---

[20] Robert Reymond, A New Systematic Theology Of The Christian Faith, Thomas Nelson Publishers, 1998, p.676

countries, God sovereignly saves and brings them to Heaven in a special area to grow before joining the rest. There are times that God shows mercy to older people who have never been introduced to the Light. According to Romans 2:12-16, God judges the heart and how people have lived their lives according to their knowledge of Him – we all are given a conscience and can choose to yield to it or ignore it.

In the Old Testament, people's faith was in Yahweh. Adam and Eve encountered the Father, Moses the Bush, Israel the Pillar and Cloud. The Old Testament teaches that God was with His people by dwelling among them in the temple rather than in them as under the new covenant (the Spirit had not yet been globally poured out, but there were exceptions). There are a few cases where the Scriptures say someone was filled with the Spirit.[21] As for babies, children and the mentally disabled, these were sovereignly regenerated by the Spirit. Those outside the Old Testament covenant, heathen babies, etc., would have been regenerated, and a little older, would have had mercy visitations (encounters or visions, dreams, with less revelation). Then in the New Covenant times, drawn by the Spirit, regenerated, and those who can believe, brought to faith in Jesus to the Father. In the New Covenant, we are the Temple indwelt by the Spirit.

Israel did have a higher calling because other nations were left out. Some from the heathen nations were saved by God's grace and mercy by an "age of accountability" or "mercy visitation". Only when the Church was really born did all who are saved come into the one high calling.

---

[21] Joshua is said to have had the Holy Spirit within him (Numbers 27:18; Deuteronomy 34:9), as were Ezekiel (Ezekiel 2:2, 3:24). Daniel (Daniel 4:8-9, 18; 5:11) and Micah (Micah 3:8).

This is also revealed in a Heaven encounter book that was written around 1909, called "40 Days in Heaven,

> *"Multitudes from heathen nations are here, their children especially, in large numbers, for they do not arrive to the age of accountability so early as in Christian lands. These are saved by virtue of the atonement, until they sin against eternal light, so thousands are gathered here well grown in years and it is these that are being taught, by these faithful servants, in preparatory regions of Paradise.*

> *"All the heathen infants are saved as well as those in civilized and Christian lands. They don't reach accountability as early as they do in more enlightened nations; hence a large number die in childhood and youth who have never known the law of God so as to bring them under condemnation, and being under the free gift of eternal life, they arrive here in very great surprise. While heathen nations are responsible to God, yet their responsibility is not so great as those of Christian lands. 'But Mother,' said Mary, 'how is it that so many of the heathen children are saved and gathered here when so many of their parents are lost?'*

> *" 'Their parents,' said Genevive, 'have reached an age of accountability through the measure of light they have. They have likewise sinned and fallen under condemnation and, following their superstitions, have died in their sins, while their children have not reached the place of enlightenment to bring them under such responsibility.'*

> *"At this I spoke and said, 'The Bible declares that, By the transgression of one man, judgement came upon all*

men to condemnation. Even, so, by the righteousness of one man the free gift came upon all men to justification of life (Romans 5:18). So, in man's beginning he is universally saved by Christ, as Paul said, again, I was alive without the law once, but the commandment came sin revived and I died' (Romans 7:9). 'Indeed,' said Genevive, 'all are alive and remain so until they receive a knowledge of God's will sufficient to bring them under responsibility, when transgression spiritual death follows. Each of these has a history of its own. They wonder with great astonishment as to who and where they are, when the angels have brought them inside the gates of paradise. The shining glory of this world is so great, many of them are completely overcome, like one on earth just awakened from a sleep filled with an enchanting dream, they are speechless with wonder.'"[22]

I agree with much of the revelation above, but I would remind the reader, *"all mankind were born in sin and have fallen short of the glory of God"* (Romans 3:23). It is not that Christ's death on the cross has wiped away all the sin of the world. It is rather that he has paid the penalty for all sin. When they are made aware of this, it is now up to each individual to choose to accept His sacrifice on their behalf through repentance, or reject it. If they reject what Jesus has done for them on their behalf, then they must be judged and defend themselves without an advocate before God Almighty. Ultimately, God is the Judge who can choose to have mercy on whomever He chooses, as He judges the heart.

Scripture tells us that mystically Jesus was slain before the foundation of the world (Revelation13:8). We don't yet fully

---

[22] Rev. Elwood Scott, 40 Days in Heaven, Published by King Edward Ltd, 2008, p. 104

understand what application this holds, but it shows from the eternal covenant (Hebrews 13:20) that God is outside time boundaries.

I stayed in India several years ago at a children's home, where the children were experiencing daily Heaven encounters. A young girl there had a severe mental disability; she needed almost everything done for her. But one day, the Lord came for her and took her life. That night in the children's encounters with Heaven, they saw her there, her body transformed, like a beautiful princess. As the children came out of their visions, gem stones exploded out of the atmosphere and covered the floor. It was a gift from her from Heaven.

Another time, I sat by my dying Grandma, who could not move and respond verbally. Before her passing moments, I asked her if she would pray a sinner's prayer with me and told her after each sentence, if she agreed, to squeeze my hand. She couldn't respond to anything, but she squeezed my hand hard each time. Our spirits can hear and respond, even if we are motionless or in a coma. I believe I will see my Grandma again in Heaven.

For Revelation 5:9 to be true, that there will be people from every tribe and nation in Heaven, one must assume that some tribes would have gone out of existence before the Gospel even got to them. Therefore, divine mercy visitations of Sovereign Salvation took place for infants and the mentally challenged.

"And have redeemed us to God by Your blood, out of every tribe, and tongue, and people, and nation." (Revelation 5:9)

"And He has made from one blood every nation of men to dwell on all the face of the earth, and has determined

their pre-appointed times and boundaries of their dwellings, so that they should seek the Lord in the hope that they might grope for Him and find Him, though He is not far from each one of us." (Acts 17:26-27)

All must come through the Spirit, through Christ to the Father; that's the only way. Jesus is the only way – the Way, the Truth and the Life! The Spirit draws, Jesus is the atonement and door to the Father (all three are God), and guide salvation. (Isaiah 63:7-10)

God can bring an angel to preach the gospel, and one day God will use an angel to preach the eternal gospel to every nation, tribe, language and people (Revelation 14:6)

What some early Church Fathers said:

"They are as infant children in whose hearts no evil originates. Nor did they know what wickedness is, but always remained as children." (Hermas 150 AD)

"Who are they that have been saved and have received the inheritance? Those, doubtless who believed God and who have continued in His love as did Caleb of Jephunneh and Joshua of Nun, and innocent children, who had no sense of evil." (Irenaeus 180 AD)

"Infancy is still yet innocent and unconscious of worldly evil." (Cyprian 250 AD)

Summary

* There is a concept of an age of accountability.

* All who are born are damaged by the fall and need to be reconciled by the Cross.

* God chose Israel to be a nation set apart with a special purpose and higher calling. This calling was to lead a people to birth Jesus and the Church, for *all* nations to enter into the higher calling.

* The unborn, those that die young, children, and the mentally impaired in Israel were sovereignly regenerated and saved.

* God did leave the gentiles "alienated from citizenship in Israel and foreigners to the covenants of promise without hope, and without God" (they didn't have daily fellowship).

* But this statement must be read in the context of - "Hope" in Acts 17:26-27. (Ephesians 2:12) - without "Hope", was not "absolute", there was the "possibility" of Hope (divine salvation) in the same time period, *"so that they should seek the Lord, in the hope that they might grope for Him and find Him, though He is not far from each one of us"* (Acts 17:27). They lived in times of ignorance (v28).

* Heathen babies, children, and the mentally impaired were sovereignly regenerated and saved, and others may have had visitation encounters.

* In Matthew 2:16, Herod ordered the killing of all the two-year-old boys. Where do you think all these babies went? Heaven.

* Israel and the Church were called to a higher calling, of which others (Heathen, those under the age of accountability or mercy) will be grafted in, over time in Heaven.

* Not everyone who knows the living God in the Old Testament comes to the knowledge through a direct commitment to the Sinai Covenant. Abimelech, Melchizedek, Rahab, Job, and others came to know God without the benefit of specific help from the chosen people.

* Yes, we must acknowledge that not all the world will be saved.

A final note: Abortion - Just because all aborted babies will be saved and in Heaven, this is not an excuse to abort them. God is against this as it attacks the image of God, in which we are created. God commanded us not to kill. It is not for us to decide when a life ends. Abortion stops a "life" from fulfilling their scroll and destiny on the earth. Those who participate and those who have abortions will be held accountable. BUT, if they ask for forgiveness, with true repentance, God will forgive them.

I heard a story about Donna Grisham, whose life was becoming suicidal because she could not forgive herself for having two abortions. One day, she was caught (translated) up to Heaven, finding herself sitting on a golden bench. Two children ran up to her, sat on her lap, and kissed her cheeks. They said, 'We forgive you, Mum. We love you." After which, she found herself back on earth.

Many who have been aborted could have been destined to bring lifesaving cures, inventions, or leave huge legacies into the earth. These destinies were prevented, yet written on their scrolls. Those babies will live on and are truly loved by the Father in Heaven.

> *"Your eyes have seen my unformed substance; And in Your book were all written the days that were ordained for me, when as yet there was not one of them. How precious also are Your thoughts to me, O God! How vast is the sum of them." (Psalm 139:16-17)*

Through the tragic death of babies, children, and the birth of the mentally impaired, their earthly days are shortened or difficult. Their Scroll has an eternal destiny of inheritance, justice, and blessings in Heaven. God's plan and His thoughts shine forth the riches of His goodness.

> *"You intended to harm me, but God intended it for good to accomplish what is now being done, the saving of many lives." (Genesis 50:20)*

The mentally impaired and severely handicapped are very precious to God. Like Jesus was a suffering servant, they too are precious gifts to us on the earth. Suffering servants - that draw out character traits of deep love and perseverance from carers' (parents' and others') hearts that wouldn't be formed without them. Both will be highly rewarded in Heaven.

I once worked in a Supermarket. One day, I saw a man being pushed in a large chair down my aisle. He was the most handicapped person I had ever seen. The Lord spoke to my heart - "See, he is a suffering servant."

> *"You who bear the vessels of the Lord... Just as many were astonished at you. So, His visage was marred more than any, and His form than the sons of man". (Isaiah 52:12,14)*

We do not talk lightly about suffering, but in the mystery, those who share greatly in Christ's sufferings are given the promise of reigning with Him, highly rewarded. Their laid-down lives, precious souls of much endurance, produces much Kingdom fruit, manifested and formed in others to serve in love.

Apart
Gardens
by the
River

In the fields of Heaven, every believer has a garden that is being cultivated by the transformation of their soul on earth.

> *"Then He said; what is the kingdom of God like? And to what shall I compare it? It is like a mustard seed, which a man took and put in his garden, and it grew and became a large tree, and the birds of the air nested in its branches." (Luke 13:18-19)*

When one is born again, they receive the imperishable seed of the spirit in their soul (1 Peter 1:23). This seed is also taken and planted in a garden in Heaven. This garden is one of many, many, in the Kingdom. We each have our own garden in Heaven, with a tree planted by the Lord in it. This tree shows the health of our soul and our fruit. Sometimes Jesus even waters our garden, bringing life in our souls on earth.

Children in India reveal from their Heaven encounters:

> *"The children love to go to their own gardens in Heaven called Apart Gardens – a place where they can meet Jesus alone. They describe lush green grass, flowers, trees with fruit, rivers, ponds and waterfalls. Some gardens have wide rivers with atolls – an outer rim of coral with water in the middle. Others have had an island given to them. Others have tree houses surrounded with birds and gardens, and some have houses surrounded by waterfalls. There is also a special tree Jesus gives them that creates a calm breeze and fills their garden."[23]*

More children report that some have lawns of smooth grass, circles of palm trees; trees bearing fruit with swirling colours of

---

[23] Angela Curtis; Talk With Me in Paradise, Kin & Kingdoms Publishing, 2019 p.46.

the rainbow, but that change continually. One child has rocks to climb that are also different colours. Some have ponds, rivers or waterfalls in their gardens.[24]

Scriptures confirm this as well,

> *"Blessed is the man who trusts the Lord, and whose hope is the Lord; For he shall be like a tree planted by the waters, which spread out its roots by the river, and will not fear when heat comes; But its leaf will be green, and will not be anxious in the year of drought, nor will cease from yielding fruit." (Jeremiah 17:7-8)*

> *"Therefore, they shall come and sing in the height of Zion, streaming to the goodness of the LORD— for wheat and new wine and oil, for the young of the flock and the herd; Their souls shall be like a well-watered garden, and they shall sorrow no more at all." (Jeremiah 31:12)*

> *"Jesus said, "Even so every good tree brings forth good fruit, but a corrupt tree brings forth evil fruit" (Matthew 7:17)*

Trees speak of us, but also spiritual "beings" in Eden:

> *"Which of the trees of Eden can be compared with you in splendour and majesty?" (Ezekiel 31:18)*

Jesus goes to His children's gardens for intimate fellowship alone to strengthen and bathe them in love.

> *"You who dwell in the gardens. The companions listen for your voice, let me hear it." (Song of Solomon 8:13)*

In the Father's Garden, His sacred Temple, there is healing, restoring and resting in His love. But we also see that there are

---

[24] Curtis, p.46,47.

areas in His Garden where there are sorrows, people's sorrows being transformed. There is the collecting of tears in the *Ocean of Tears* (Psalm 56:8), and the prayers and tears of Jesus and the Father drop into this Ocean too (Jeremiah 13:17). Many sit by this Ocean and pray with intercession. The Father's Garden is a place of love and a Garden of sorrows being used for spiritual advancements for the Kingdom.

B. Berrakhot 59a says that God's tears flow down his fingers into an ocean pool that builds spiritual power to be released on earth.

It is interesting that as on earth, so in Heaven,

> *"Now in the place where He was crucified there was a garden, and in the garden a new tomb in which no one had yet been laid." (John 19:41)*

As Jesus suffered in a garden of sorrows on earth, it is almost an example that we will at times find ourselves in the Father's Garden of sorrows, in the cave (tomb), working out soul issues to be transformed into glory, all while being embraced in the Father's love.

> *"And we know that all things work together for good to those who love God, to those who are called according to His purpose." (Romans 8:28)*

Body Parts
Room

For many, hearing about a 'body parts' room in Heaven can be hard to believe. But one of the young ladies on the campus where I stayed in India has seen this room. This young lady was born with one arm missing from the elbow down. When she used to get caught up to Heaven in worship in vision, it was amazing to sit and watch her move. In Heaven, she would be doing things, and on earth, it almost looked like she believed she had two full arms. She once said that her 'arm' is in Heaven, and it is possible for it to appear on her, on earth, manifested, but would take great intercession to access. I have no reason to doubt the claims of these young ones.

"Every good gift and every perfect gift is from above, and comes down from the Father of lights, with whom there is no variation or shadow of turning." (James 1:17)

There are store-houses or treasury rooms near the throne that store many things. Each of them is guarded by angels, and Jewish tradition says there is the treasury of rain, of ice and snow, the treasury of clouds, the treasury of peace, of blessings, and of dew with which God will revive the dead. There is also the treasury of merits and comfort.[25] These warehouses near the throne store many things, even souls that have not yet been born.

It's interesting to note that Robert Liadon, when he was caught up to Heaven, was shown the body parts building, and Jesus told him that these parts were 'unclaimed blessings'. Now, James 1:17 tells us every perfect gift is from above and comes down, and Jewish tradition tells us there is a storehouse called the treasury of blessings. And we are told that the treasuries of

---

[25] Howard Schwartz, p. 169

blessings and of dew are used to revive the dead. So, are the body parts in the treasury of blessings?

If God can manifest stones, if He can manifest healing leaves from Heaven, then why not body parts? There are degrees of healing that can be ministered. Sometimes it can just be a frequency change from overshadowing glory that brings healing. Other times it can be Jesus giving a spoken word or using spit. Other times Angels can bring spiritual ointments and balms and infuse them in us, and at other times 'body parts' can come down from the treasury of blessings.

Ways God heals:

* Through the work of the Cross, and the Blood of Jesus. (1 Peter 2:24)

* The spoken words of Jesus. (John 5:8)

* God releasing and shining spiritual light which changes the fabric of the structure of reality by frequencies, and restores to new the material world. (Acts 9:3)

* The faith-filled prayers of the Saints. (James 5:16)

* By faith, eating spiritual tonics, and healing leaves. (Revelation 22:1-2 – speaks of fruit (tonics) and healing leaves (medicine)).

There are other ways God heals and brings strength to His children. Every believer has a garden in Heaven that is continually growing and changing based on the condition of our soul's health. Sometimes when we are struggling on earth, Jesus will water our garden with living water, and on earth, life and strength will rise up in our souls. I have experienced this many times.

> *"The Lord will guide you continually, and satisfy your soul in drought, and strengthen your bones. You shall be like a well-watered garden, and like a spring of water whose waters do not fail." (Isaiah 58:11)*

Bill Johnson shares his experience:

> *"Years ago, one of our students had an encounter with the Lord. It was really quite bizarre. In heaven, she actually saw this room with spare body parts. You say, "Well, that doesn't exist in heaven." I don't know. I haven't seen it. But she did. And she was with Chris ministering down in Santa Rosa, I think it was. And a gal came up that was in a head-on collision, had really messed up her legs. Used to be a dancer and had very little function.... four or five, maybe six people have seen the same thing. And since then, we have been seeing creative miracles. So, this girl comes up to her talking about her accident, and she needed a miracle, and she says, "I don't even have a kneecap!" Well, the gal who'd seen the spare parts room in Heaven says, "Well, I'll get one for you." That's like, that's got to be like the ultimate response ever! "Well, I'll get one for you." She reaches her arm up like this, she brings it down, lays hands on the knees and within fifteen minutes, she has a new knee cap."[26]*

---

[26] Bill Johnson - You Are a Gate Of Heaven - part 2
https://www.youtube.com/watch?v=XVVQV70y1Es (accessed 19/01/2022)

Another Heaven encounter,

> *"In this room was a counter like what you see at a catalog store, and there were shelves all along the walls and a beautiful conveyer system like what hotels have to check coats with. The only difference was that these hangers had body parts on them. There were hangers with different leg bones, arm bones, containers with organs in them and even a box with body part names written on papers that you would hand in to an attendant. I was fascinated and in awe with the whole vision and not at all scared."*[27]

It was medically verified that Gary Wood died[28]. He went to heaven and saw the "body parts room" full of replacements waiting for people who need them.

Tony Kemps testimony:

> *An angel came to me, and he had sandy brown hair. He took me up into the heavens. I was taken to the body parts room and there on the table and hanging were literally hearts, kidneys, bones, livers, different body parts, fingers, eyes, ears, all kinds of body parts. And there were two angels assigned to me. One was an angel that would give me a revelation concerning healing, miracles and other matters, and the other was an angel that would minister with me in the area of miracles.*[29]

---

[27] Brenda Gale Thompson, Spare Parts Room In Heaven – posted 12 September 2011 https://greatcommissionhow2s.blogspot.com/2011/09/spare-parts-room-in-heaven.html (accessed 19/01/2022)

[28] https://sidroth.org/television/tv-archives/gary-wood-2012/

[29] http://sidroth.org/sites/default/files/IS565Transcript_Kemp.pdf

Heidi Baker,

> *"Heidi had a vision of a room in heaven that was full of body parts... She saw ears and human hearts and gallbladders... God said to her: 'When I tell you, you can have access to this room."[30]*

Robert Liardon claims that he toured Heaven when he was only eight years old. He said Jesus is five feet eleven to six feet tall and has sandy brown hair that is "not too long and not too short." He saw storage buildings containing body parts that are waiting for saints.

> *"We walked a little farther—and this is the most important, and perhaps the strangest part of my story. I saw three storage houses 500 to 600 yards from the Throne Room of God. They were very long and very wide. There may be more, but I only saw three. We walked into the first. As Jesus shut the front door behind us, I looked around the interior in shock!*

> *"On one side of the building were exterior parts of the body. Legs hung from the wall, but the scene looked natural, not grotesque. On the other side of the building were shelves filled with eyes: green ones, brown ones, blue ones, and so forth. This building contained all of the parts of the human body that people on earth need, but Christians have not realized these blessings are waiting in heaven. There is no place else in the universe for these parts to go except right here on earth; no one else needs them.*

> *"Jesus said to me, 'These are the unclaimed blessings. This building should not be full. It should be emptied.*

---

[30] Cassandra Soars *Love Like Fire*, Charisma House (April 5, 2016) page 44-45

You should come in here with faith and get the needed parts for you, and the people you will come in contact with that day.' The unclaimed blessings are there in those storehouses—all of the parts of the body people might need: hundreds of new eyes, legs, skin, hair, eardrums—they are all there. All you have to do is go in and get what you need by the arm of faith, because it is there.

"You do not have to cry and beg God to make the part you need. Just go get it. The doors to the storehouses are never locked. They are always open for those who need to go in. We should empty those buildings. Sometimes when we pray, an angel will leave heaven to bring us the answer—just as the angel did for Daniel (Daniel 10:12) but can't get through right away. Daniel kept praying and fasting for 21 days, until he got his answer. Because of his persistence in prayer, the angel was able to get through the demonic hindrances of the second heavens, where the principalities, powers, and rulers of darkness of this world live. (Ephesians 6:12.) What would have happened if Daniel had not kept praying and 'pressing in' to God for his answer? The angel might not have gotten through the warfare with the Prince of Persia (Daniel 10:13), and Daniel would not have received an answer."[31]

God's promises are 'Yes and Amen' (2 Corinthians 1:20). This means that He stands by His promises; you can trust Him to fulfil them. There are measures of promises we can access according to our faith and intercession. God can answer our prayers in different ways or have multiple paths that can unfold.

---

[31] https://www.nairaland.com/1237463/storehouses-heaven (accessed 26/01/2022)

At one level, God can strengthen us, He can heal us, and then at another level, if we are persistent, we can access the higher realms, places, like the body parts room. God will always give us what we need and grace to walk through what we have.

All God's promises are good, but not every promise has been given to each person. We can access every good promise that has been written for our individual days on earth. For example, if God has decided that someone will be single all their lives, they will be given many wonderful promises they can access, but the promise of a soul mate will not unfold. All God's promises are, 'Yes and Amen,' but not all people get the same gifts in life, but God gives us the grace to walk out His purposes.

> *"These all died in faith, not having received the promises, but having seen them afar off were assured of them, embraced them and confessed that they were strangers and pilgrims on the earth." (Hebrews 11:13)*

In Hebrews 11:13, all the promises were good, but they did not receive 'some promises', this side of eternity. All God's promises are good, but in God's wise, mysterious counsel, they have been held back for a greater promise or blessing in Heaven. And in some cases, as with Abraham, those promises take time, longer than our lifetime, to be fulfilled.

> *"Your eyes saw my substance, being yet unformed, And in Your book, they were written, the days fashioned for me, when as yet there were none of them." (Psalm 139:16)*

When it comes to healing, never give up praying for God's grace. His love and mercy are a million times deeper than you can comprehend. His mercies are new every day.

Scripture hints that it is possible to bring down body parts from Heaven,

> *"Now faith is the substance of things hoped for, the evidence of things not seen. For by it, the elders obtained a good testimony. By faith, we understand that the worlds were framed by the word of God, so that the things which are seen were not made of things which are visible." (Hebrews 11:1-3)*

> *"And I have put My words in your mouth; I have covered you with the shadow of My hand, that I may plant the heavens, lay the foundations of the earth, and say to Zion, 'You are My people.'" (Isaiah 51:16)*

We are told that by faith, if we hope, the "substance" from the unseen realm can "form" into the seen material word on earth; that we can plant, graft the gifts (body parts) of Heaven into the earth.

It's not hard for body parts to be "formed". God formed our inward parts, and it's not hard to believe that there is a place in Heaven that stores these parts. God loves to be creative; everything is more complex than it 'just' appears by a word. There is always great detail and processes in Heaven. God speaks the "substance forms" into being, and these are stored, ready to be called upon and downloaded, and knitted into the earth realm.

> *"For You formed my inward parts; You covered me in my mother's womb." (Psalm 139:13)*

Donna Rigney says,

> *"There is this place in Heaven called the Hall of Miracles. And it is an enormous hall, miles and miles*

long, and its gold, gold floor with beautiful chandeliers, there's diamonds hanging from the ceiling. And down this hall are doorways, all doorways. And so the Lord brought me there... So I went in the first doorway, the first doorway on the left was a room full of body parts. There were legs; there were arms; there were eyeballs; there were ears. There were all the things that God's children here on earth would need. He got them ready. At the great revival that's coming, He's going to empty that room, and it will be pulled to earth.[32]

In Ecclesiastes 11:5. Solomon wrote,

"As you do not know what is the way of the wind, or how the bones grow in the womb of her who is with child, so you do not know the works of God who makes everything."

---

[32] https://divinerevelations.com.ng/donna-rigney-chamber-of-despair-in-hell-hall-of-miracles-in-heaven-hearing-gods-voice/ (accessed 26/01/2022)

The
Stables
of *Eden*

Near the Garden of Eden are Jesus' Heavenly Stables, where
thousands of horses are tended to. The stables are on the
Mountain of the Lord, and house the Lord's Army - His battle
horses.

> *"Blow the Trumpet in Zion, and sound an alarm in My
> Holy Mountain... The land is like the garden of Eden
> before them, and behind them a desolate wilderness.
> Surely nothing escapes them. Their appearance is like
> the appearance of horses, And, like swift steeds, so they
> run. With a noise like chariots over mountaintops they
> leap. Like the noise of a flaming fire that devours the
> stubble, Like a strong people set in battle array."
> (Excerpts from Joel 2:1-5)*

The Children in India were shown the stables in their
Heaven encounters:

> *"One visit to Heaven, Chris and Jess were taken by an
> angel to see the heavenly stables. This is Jesus' horse,
> the angel said, standing next to a gigantic white
> stallion, bigger than any horse the girls had seen. They
> walked over and reached up to pat its nose. 'Hello,
> Chris' said, 'What's your name?' Jess asked. The
> horse didn't reply, just bent down so they could rub its
> head. He shook his head and his mane flew around him,
> was an impressive sight, considering his size. 'Come
> on. I have other horses to show you,' the angel said.
> They walked some distance before they came to a huge
> open area. There were thousands of horses with golden
> chariots attached, lined up in formation as far as they
> could see. 'What are the horses doing?' Chris asked.
> 'They are waiting to do the Lord's work.'"[33]*

---

[33] Angela Curtis, Talk With Me in Paradise, Kin & Kingdom, 2019, p.124

Scripture tells us,

> *"They climb the wall like men of war. Everyone marches in formation, and they do not break ranks. They do not push one another; Every one marches in his own column. Though they lunge between the weapons, they are not cut down." (Joel 2:7-8)*

Donna Rigney has also been to the heavenly stables,

> *" 'Today, I am going to take you to a stable in Heaven,' He explained. We climbed through the clouds above into the soft blue sky. It felt like only seconds passed, and we were walking into a large, red stable. Stalls line either side of the long passageway. The Lord led me from stall to stall, where I saw the most fantastic horses imaginable; one was all white, another shiny black with white hooves, another was chestnut brown in colour... Angels helped us by unbolting each stall; it was apparent they were the caretakers of the Lord's treasured horses."*[34]

Every believer has their own horse that they can use to ride up to Heaven as a way of Heavenly transport. When I experienced my Heaven encounter, I found myself caught out of my body riding on a white horse to Heaven with angels riding horses beside me.

What fascinates me the most is that my friends in the jungles of India have encountered details identical to other people's accounts on the other side of the world. Those friends have never read or heard of Donna Rigney, but they saw the chestnut horse,

---

[34] Donna Rigney, The Gory of God Revealed, Its Supernatural, 2021

"In the distance, I saw a radiant, white horse - a horse of perfection. I knew without asking that it belonged to Jesus. I watched it and it watched me. It acknowledged me with a nod, and I nodded back. Then my attention was caught by the sound of hooves and laughing behind me. I turned to see the Holy Spirit (Pillar of light) leading an elegant chestnut horse with a silky mane and a long beautiful fringe that hung down to its big brown eye. The horse was very tall. 'Hi, my name is Noble,' he said. 'Noble is your horse, Jan,' the Holy Spirit said. 'Hi Noble, I'm Jan,' I said. Noble bent his two front legs and kneeled on the grass so I could climb on." [35]

Scripture tells us more,

"And Elisha prayed and said, 'Lord, I pray, open his eyes that he may see.' Then the Lord opened the eyes of the young man, and he saw. And behold, the mountain was full of horses and chariots of fire all around Elisha." (2 Kings 6:17)

"On earth, as it is in Heaven" shows us how things are connected between the Heavenly and Earthly realms.

King Solomon had many stalls made for his large number of chariot horses and cavalry (1 Kings 4:26, 2 Chronicles 1,14; 9,25).

Sometimes horses in Scripture speak of God's power and strength.

"In the *Song of Solomon*, the spectacular beauty of the horse is used as an image to portray the comeliness of the beloved.

---

[35] Curtis, p126.

The bejewelled Egyptian mare was by then well known to the Jews, resulting in this encomium: *I compare you, my love, to a mare among Pharaoh's chariots (Song of Solomon 1:9).* The theme of the great strength of the horse is also orchestrated in Isaiah when the prophet remembers the Mighty Hand that led Israel from Egypt through the river Nile: *Who led them through the depths? Like a horse in the desert, they did not stumble (Isaiah 63:13).*

King Solomon systematically equipped himself with more horses. The proliferation of chariots and horses by King Solomon is a recurring theme in the Book of Kings: *And Solomon had forty thousand stalls of horse for his chariots, and twelve thousand horsemen (1 Kings 4:26).* "[36]

Scripture tells us that Jesus will be returning on a white horse with the army of Heaven,

> *"And I saw heaven opened, and behold a white horse; and he that sat upon him was called Faithful and True, and in righteousness he doth judge and make war."* *(Revelation 19:11)*

> *"And the armies of heaven, arrayed in fine linen, white and pure, were following him on white horses. From his mouth comes a sharp sword with which to strike down the nations, and he will rule them will a rod of iron. He will tread the winepress of the fury of the wrath of God the Almighty..."* *(Revelation 19:18)*

---

[36] https://jewishcurrents.org/the-horse-in-jewish-religious-text (accessed 25/01/2022)

The
Dark Cloud
of the Fear of God

The Father sits on the throne, clothed with a cloud of white mist. This cloud is the spirit of glory, Holy Spirit that covers the image of the Father. Around the throne and over the throne shines the seven rings of the colours of the rainbow. These rings of light are the seals of light of the full image of God that we must be conformed to and reflect.

The seven spirits of God stand around the throne, each being a tutor of one of the seals of God's image. To be a true king, a mature son, one must yield to them all. The fear of the Lord completes them all. The cloud acts as an insulation, veiling God's glory and the Father's face and image. At the base of the throne, you can just see the Father's feet, and all around is paved with sapphire stone. Further out from the throne, many fall on their faces in worship.

As one goes down the mountain, one finds a forest cave that leads under the throne to the Father's Garden. Deeper still, ones come to the cloud of His presence, a cloud of mist. You do not enter this cloud until you are drawn and also called. Under the throne, which is also connected above, this cloud is the Dark Cloud of God. Those called into the cloud for a season, sit in a mist in deep intercession. This realm is the 'realm of the fear of the Lord'. It is so holy that you feel the pressure of the fear of the Lord, the terror of the Lord. It is a place the other attributes of God are not felt. It is a place that is uncomfortable; everything is heightened. But those taken on this journey must go there for a season, sit in darkness, and be transfigured by the weight of God's presence. It is the seal of understanding the "Awe" and "Terror", reverence, absolute holiness, knowledge, of the fear of God. To understand the full glory of God, one must understand the absolute fullness of His reverence.

"The Lord said that He would dwell in the thick darkness." (1 Kings 8:12).

The word darkness means to dread or be afraid, to fear.

Under the throne, one sits under the "shadow" of the Almighty.

"He who dwells in the secret place of the Most High shall abide under the shadow of the Almighty." (Psalm 91:1)

Moses went into the cloud and also saw God face to face. Those taken on this journey, who have been transfigured to understand, can walk deeper through the cloud, climb the steps, and stand face-to-face with the Father in all His glory. One will be clothed with a robe and a ring and be a complete king.

"For now we see in a mirror dimly, but then face to face. Now I know in part, but then shall I know just as I also am known." (1 Corinthians 13:12)

Geographical
Landscape Map

The entrance to the Father's Garden is under the throne, a little down the Mountain of the Lord, an opening, a Cave that leads through a forest (Psalm 27:5 - Zephaniah 2:6-7)

(Interesting -the Cave of Machpelah, the burial site of Adam and Eve, was considered the entrance to the Garden of Eden)[37]

> *"Like an apple tree among the trees of the 'forest', so is my lover among the sons." (Song of Solomon 2:3)*

As one comes out of the forest, they come to a large meadow, gardens, and many pathways leading to righteous places. (Psalm 23:2)

Solomon is a type/shadow of God in His Garden. He was a master gardener; he made 'cedars as plentiful as sycamore trees' (1 King 10:27). He planted vineyards, gardens and parks, and planted in them all kinds of fruit trees, and made ponds of water to irrigate a forest of growing trees. (Ecclesiastes 2:4-6)

On the west bank of the Kidron valley, east of the city, was the 'Kings Garden', watered by the Gihon spring. The royal garden of Jerusalem, the city of God, was the earthly copy of the garden above in Eden.

At the end of the meadow in Heaven is the Father's Garden, and to enter it, one crosses over a bridge. From this Garden, many paths lead to many seashores. (Zephaniah 2:6)

We know of a few of them, the Ocean of Tears, and the Ocean of Love, that the children play on.

The Ocean of Tears is also an area where great intercession (prayers of saints in Heaven) takes place (as seats are overlooking that Ocean and the forming tears and sounds) for

---

[37] Midrash 92:6 – Tree of Souls, The Mythology of Judaism, p.334.

the many tears that are being collected from earth (Psalm 56:8). It's a Garden of love, sorrows and victories.

As tears form into precious stones in the Ocean, they are collected and mounted in the Wall of Remembrance (Psalm 56:8).

> *"I will make your battlements of rubies, your gates of sparkling jewels, and all your walls of precious stones." (Isaiah 54:12)*

In 'Ein Ya Akeov Hotza At Sefa', it says, "He places them (tears) in His House of Treasure in order to use them for the resurrection of life." The precious stones mounted in the wall are the heavenly copy of the Wailing Wall of the Temple on earth. The Talmud says, "Whosoever sheds tears at the death of a good man, the Holy One counts them and stores them away in His Treasure House. You have counted my wanderings, put my tears in your flasks, and are they not already in your ledger?"

It is the place Jesus goes to intercede for us, sitting by the Ocean of Tears, *"He is able to save to the uttermost those who come to God through Him, since he always lives to make intercession for them."* (Hebrews 7:25)

It is interesting to note that the field chosen by Isaac, on the Mountain where his father Abraham had bound him as a sacrifice, became the site of the Holy Temple, God's House of prayer for all nations. Similarly, inside the Cave under the throne, in the sacred Temple by the Ocean of Tears, is a place (house - the Cave is a house) of prayer for all nations, where prayer sacrifices go up.

> *"Blessed are those who dwell in Your house; they will still be praising You. Blessed is the man whose strength is in You, whose heart is set on pilgrimage. As they pass*

*through the Valley of Baca, they make it a spring; the
rain also covers it with pools. They go from strength
to strength; each one appears before God in Zion."
(Psalm 84:4-7)*

In the ancient world, a Cave inside a Mountain was
considered a sacred Temple. Under the throne, in the Father's
Garden is a sacred intimate Holy place.

Revelation 21:22 says that John saw no (structural) temple
(in heaven) because the Lord's presence dwelling there, forms
the temple not built with hands. He does not dwell in temples
made with hands (Acts 17:24), but inside the cave is His sacred
dwelling (considered a temple).

The Father has an intimate Swing in the Garden for mystical
rest, transformation, and embracing pure love. This Swing not
only has healing power, but creativity and fruit-producing power
for expanding the Kingdom. The Father moves from a place of
perfect peace and rest!

If one goes deeper under the throne, one walks into the Dark
mist of the presence of the Holy fear of the Lord. (1 Kings 8:12)

Near the throne, almost like stepping stones to the throne,
in the Father's Garden are 'the Stones of Fire'. These stones are
so mystical and powerful, not much is known about them. But
these stones speak of the revelation of our purpose and destiny.

*"You were in Eden, the garden of God - You walked
back and forth in the midst of the stones of fire."
(Ezekiel 28:13-14)*

Frankincense ascends and descends around the throne as
incense. As it descends, it can be smelled below in the Father's
Garden. Young lions are seen roaming around the Garden.

"Until the day breaks, and the shadow flee away, I will go my way to the mountain of myrrh, and to the hill of frankincense." (Song of Solomon 6:6)

"Come with me from Lebanon, my spouse, with me from Lebanon. Look from the top of Amana, from the top of Senir and Hermon, from the lions' dens, from the mountains of the leopards." (Song of Solomon 4:8)

"A garden enclosed... Spikenard and saffron, calamus and cinnamon, with all trees of frankincense, myrrh and aloes, with all the chief spices. A fountain of gardens, a well of living waters, and streams from Lebanon." (Song of Solomon 4:12,14,15)

One of the young children I met in India describes his Heaven encounter with his lion, Jani:

"My lion and I walked to a special place to pray. Afterwards, we picked fruit and gave it to each other to eat. We heard the trees and flowers worshipping and turned to find Jesus coming towards us. After inquiring about our day, Jesus led us to a different worship place where He put a crown on all the boys and girls. Then He took us to a waterfall with a slide."[38]

In 1 Kings 10:22 and 2 Chronicles 9:21, we read of monkeys and peacocks being imported to Israel by King Solomon. G.K. Beales, in his book, *A New Testament Biblical Theology: The unfolding of the Old Testament in the New*, makes the connection that the animals found in Israel on earth are also found in "Eden above" – Heaven.

A child's Heaven encounter reveals:

"I love Hullah, the monkey. He is cheeky and always laughing. He's black, has a white face and is over three

---

[38] Curtis, p.124

feet tall. When we are in the garden, he jumps and swings through the branches from tree to tree."[39]

"He who has an ear, let him hear what the Spirit says to the churches. To him who overcomes I will give to eat from the tree of life, which is in the midst of the Paradise of God." (Revelation 2:7).

It is a reward (Revelation 22:12) to those who overcome to have an enhanced intimacy with God.

---

[39] Curtis, p.41

Peace

Like the River

"For thus says the LORD: "Behold, I will extend peace to her like a river, and the glory of the nations like an overflowing stream; and you shall nurse, you shall be carried upon her hip, and bounced upon her knees." (Isaiah 66:12)

"Rejoice with Jerusalem, and be glad with her, that you may feed and be satisfied with the consolation of her bosom. That you may drink deeply and be delighted with the abundance of her glory." (Isa 66;10-11)

On earth, as in Heaven. From the throne above the Mountain, in Heaven, God's spirit/river flows down through the New Jerusalem into Eden. This river splits off into many streams, little rivers, and estuaries. It is a place where people can go, sit, float in the river to feel God's presence, and flow like being on a hip of a mother being comforted. It is also a place where people are told to drink the water because it gives one's soul powerful peace. People are told to drink deeply to be satisfied and feel safe. Many people are caught up to sit and drink the peace glory river.

By faith on earth, we can pray for God's Spirit, the river of peace as His river is inside us. But also, Peace angels can come around us and radiate God's presence over you, shielding you from fear and attacks like a pulsating dome of security. We must also guard our minds and think on Heavenly things.

"And the peace of God, which surpasses all understanding, will guard your hearts and your minds in Christ Jesus." (Philippians 4:7)

"What you have learned and received and heard and seen in me—practice these things, and the God of peace will be with you." (Philippians 4:9)

Come, Holy Spirit, wash over ME!

The children in India have been to the river of peace in their Heaven encounters:

> *"God's glory is in the water of Heaven, especially in the River of Life. The children often visit to play and swim. From their testimonies, the River of Life flows from the throne of God and appears to separate into many rivers. They flow into lakes and oceans, watering and feeding all the plants and gardens of heaven along the way."*[40]

> *"One branch of the River of Life I called the Peace River. The angels encourage the children to drink the water there so they can experience the peace of heaven. There are always people there. Some soak in the river to experience God's peace as it washes over them."*[41]

> *"Oh, that you had paid attention to my commandments! Then your peace would have been like a river, and your righteousness like the waves of the sea."* (Isaiah 48:18)

Peace is the essence of the Kingdom of God. The Kingdom is governed by peace. Wherever the peace of God takes ground, that realm is ordered and established. The government of God and His peace are inseparable (Isaiah 9:6-7). Jesus said that the peace He gives is not of this world (John 14:27), and that we must go and drink. Jesus is the "Prince of Peace", and the rivers in Eden are the dwelling of His presence, living water. We are told to soak in God's peace, and our lives will be calm and ordered and governed. His peace and love drive out all fear, anger and disorder.

---

[40] Curtis, p 53.
[41] Curtis, p.54

The
Father's
Friend

"No longer do I call you servants, for a servant does not know what his master is doing, but I have called you friends. For all things that I heard from My Father I have made known to you." (John 15:15)

The most amazing truth that lights up this passage is that Jesus has made known everything He has heard the Father say. So, when Jesus says, but I have called you friends, the Father, in reality, has called us friends. And what do friends do? They spend time together.

Many have thought it is impossible to be friends with the Father (from a couple of passages). With Jesus, yes, but not the Father. Likewise, some have said you cannot see the Father and live. But the truth is, Moses saw the Father, and Scripture tells us we can be the Father's friend.

"He who loves purity of heart, and has grace on his lips. The King will be his friend." (Proverbs 22:11)

"Blessed are the pure in heart, for they shall see God." (Matthew 5:8)

Many of us have put the Father at a great distance and believed we can only have fellowship with Jesus, but this is not the case. The Father is not some floating, invisible mind/force. He is a Person. Through the cross of Jesus, we now have access to the Father. Those who pursue the Father will encounter the Father.

The Father longs to meet us in His garden. He longs for us to know Him and see Him face to face (1 Corinthians13:12). Those who love the Father will visit the Father in Heaven as a friend. Even now, people are being caught up in encounters to see the Father. The Father loves His children and wants to talk, play, and fellowship with His children.

Adam walked with God - the Father. (Genesis 3:8)

Enoch walked with God - the Father. (Genesis 5:24)

Moses saw God the Father face to face. (Exodus 33:11)

Paul knew he would see the Father face to face. (1 Corinthians 13:12)

Now, one cannot just casually hang out with the Father, for most who are caught up to the throne can't even get near Him because His presence is breath-taking and overwhelming. It takes a process of becoming like Him; we see Him dimly, then face to face. (1 Corinthians 13:12)

With Jesus, the Apostle John fell on his face as dead, but Jesus said, *"Do not be afraid; I am the First and the Last." (Revelation 1:17)*

With the Father, many will not be able to stand near the throne, but they will meet Him face to face as a friend over time. (Proverbs 22:11)

> *"For through Him (Jesus), we both have access by one Spirit to the Father." (Ephesians 2:18)*

Wendy Alec captures this beautifully,

> *"She continued alone up the nave, straight towards the throne and brilliance of white light. In my earthly mindset, I became uneasy, thinking at any moment, surely, she should stop or surely some angelic being would stop her stead, but she continued walking towards the throne. She walked directly into brilliance of light into the center of where the Father's outline was, dimly, dimly visible, until her entire form disap-*

peared. 'Who is she,' I asked in awe. Jesus smiled, tenderly moved, 'She is My Father's friend,' he whispered. "[42]

As we close this chapter, I leave us with the words of the great seventh-century Puritan Scholar, John Owen,

> *"How few of the saints are experimentally acquainted with the privilege of holding immediate communion with the Father in love! With what anxious, doubtful thoughts do they look upon him! What fears, what questionings are there, of his good will and kindness! At best, many think that there is no sweetness at all in him towards us, but what is purchased at the high price of the blood of Jesus. It is true, that alone is the way of communication; but the free fountain and spring of all is in the bosom of the Father. "[43]*

It is in the bosom of the Father that we belong, purchased by His Son, revealing Him, drawing us into Him. Jesus came out of the Father's bosom (John 1:18) and redeemed us so that we can go through the veil of the Holy Spirit of Glory, to sit upon the Father's Bosom (heart), I in Him, and Him in Me.

---

[42] Alec, p.130

[43] Of Communion with God the Father, Son, and Holy Ghost (1657), in The Works of John Owen, ed. W.H.Goold (Edinburgh; Johnstone and Hunter, 1850-53).

A CALL TO RECKONING

Has this book stirred you? Would you like to commit your life to God and follow Jesus as your Saviour?

I would suggest you read the following scriptures:

John 14:6 - *"Jesus said to him, "I am the way, the truth and the life; no man comes to the Father, except through me."*

Romans 3:23 - *"For all have sinned, and come short of the glory of God."*

John 3:16 - *"For God so loved the world that He gave his only begotten Son, that whosoever believes in Him, will not die, but have eternal life."*

1 Corinthians 15:3,4 - *"Christ died for our sins; He was buried and rose again on the third day according to the scriptures."*

Ephesians 2:7 - *"For by grace you are saved through faith; and that not of yourselves; it is the gift of God."*

John 1:12,13 - *"As many as received Him, to them He gave the power to become sons of God, even to them that believe on His name; which were born not of blood, nor the will of the flesh, nor the will of man, but of God."*

Now you will understand that none of us can enter Heaven on our own merits, but only through believing that Jesus Christ has already paid the penalty for your wrongdoings by dying on the cross for you. It's as simple as talking to God, but if you're not sure how, read Psalm 51 aloud, as it is a prayer David prayed to God when he'd sinned.

Now, get your own copy of the Bible (King James Version, New American Standard versions are pretty accurate translations, but NIV could be easier to read). And find a Bible-believing fellowship in your community who can help you grow.

BIBLIOGRAPHY

Alec, W. (2013). *Visions of Heaven.* Warboys Publishing Ltd.

Carlebach, S. (2004). *Lamed Vav,* Israel Book Shop

Clayton, I. (2014). *Realms of the Kingdom, Volume One,* Seraph Creative Publishers.

Curtis, A. (2019). *Talk With Me in Paradise.* Kin & Kingdom Books.

Fellows, R. (2019). *Granny Rainbow Shekinah,* WordWyze Publishing.

Fellows, R. (2021). *Heaven Through the Eyes of Children,* WordWyze Publishing.

Geisler, N. (2003). *Systematic Theology, Volume Two, God, Creation,* Bethany House Publishers.

Hardinge, L. (2011). *Stones of Fire,* American Christian Ministries.

Nash, R. (1999). *When a Baby Dies,* Zondervan Publishing House.

Owen, J. (1657). *Of Communion with God the Father, Son, and Holy Ghost,* ed. W.H. Goold (Edinburgh; Johnstone and Hunter, 1850-53

Reymond, R. (1998). *A New Systematic Theology of the Christian Faith,* Thomas Nelson Publishers.

Rigney, D. (2021). *Glory of God Revealed,* It's Supernatural.

Schwartz, H. (2004). *Tree of Souls, The Mythology of Judaism,* Oxford University Press.

Scott, E. (2008). *40 Days in Heaven,* King Edward Ltd.

Soars, C. (2016). *Love Like Fire*, Charisma House.

Webb, R.A. (1907). *The Theology of Infant Salvation*, Presbyterian Committee of Publication

Palanquin - [noun] a conveyance formerly used especially in eastern Asia usually for one person that consists of an enclosed litter borne on the shoulders of men by means of poles.
https://www.merriam-webster.com/dictionary/palanquin

An image of a hammock-like palanquin:
https://external-preview.redd.it/effjnQQ2N_oea39VtVyBgHgVCy8E4J068YSa50-UlVY.jpg

NOTES

Other books by Richard Fellows, available online or direct from the author – richfellows@hotmail.com

Wilderness Like Eden (2019) ISBN 978-0-648-58830-6

The supernatural appearing of gemstones from Heaven, around the world, is on the increase as faithful Christians worship God and cry out for the joining of Heaven and earth. What is the phenomenon? How is it related to the God of the Bible?

In Wilderness Like Eden, these questions are addressed in the light of God's Heavenly Kingdom intimately clothing Eden, the Bride and the Sons of God – their functions and callings in the earth.

Granny Rainbow Shekinah (2019)
ISBN 978-0-648-58832-0

Throughout history, God has revealed Himself in His creation. In The Garden of Eden, he visited earth in Theophanies in the Old Testament, in the incarnation of Jesus, and also in disguise, after His resurrection and ascension into Heaven. But what of the Holy Spirit, what is His image and likeness? What is the Holy Spirit's "form" and essence as the Spirit of Glory? In Granny Rainbow Shekinah, these questions and more are addressed. Come on a journey as we go behind the veil!

Heaven Through the Eyes of Children (2021)

ISBN 978-0-648-58834-4

When a Theologian encounters Heaven himself, his heart is opened to believe like a child, and is challenged by a small community of children in the jungles of India experiencing visions of Heaven. Hidden in the remote mountains, a remarkable outpouring of the Holy Spirit touched a community and revealed the reality of Jesus and His Kingdom in Heaven.

This is a Theologian's journey of analysing the geographical landscape of Heaven based on their testimonies. From the eyes of children, through the mind of a Theologian, the truth is revealed.

Heaven THROUGH THE EYES OF CHILDREN

Richard Fellows

Some other books you may be interested in –

also co-published by WordWyze Publishing and presented here with permission of the author, Richard Fellows.

Kat Wassenaar takes us on a personal journey of how God wants us to be free of unforgiveness and offences, and how we can be healed of mental illness and the traumas we carry with us. Biblically based, and with encouragement and tools, this book will challenge and guide you. Freedom awaits!

Forgiveness (2020) ISBN – 978-0-473-54007-4

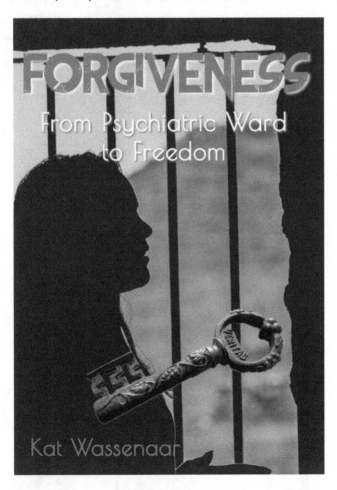

Justine Orme is fast becoming a well-known NZ author. Her first two books in the *I Am Beryl Chronology* were well-received world-wide. These are the first 2 in a chronology of 5 books telling the story of Creation and the Bible through the 'eyes' of the Beryl stone, mentioned 8 times throughout the Bible.

In The Beginning – I AM BERYL CHRONOLOGY, Book 1 (2018) ISBN 978-0-473-45197-4

A Stone in my Sandal - I AM BERYL CHRONOLOGY, Book 2 (2020) ISBN 978-0-473-50407-6

25 to Life is Justine's personal story, told in novel form, of how Jesus can heal from sexual abuse, which can be like a life-sentence to anyone who has experienced it. There is HOPE!

25 TO LIFE (2019) ISBN 978-0-473-48009-7

Don't miss out on Book 3 of the *I Am Beryl Chronology* – To Shula with Love – due in 2022!

Justine Orme's latest book, *Arabella* is on its way to being the nest best-seller! People from around the world are being blessed! Get your copy now!

Arabella is a parable of the Christian life as it should be, where intimacy with Jesus is normal; where Believers are fully aware of the Spiritual realm around them, and know their place and authority in Christ.

ARABELLA ISBN 978-0-473-60368-7 (2021)

Books are available worldwide online or order from any bookstore or library or direct from justineorme@justineormeauthor.com

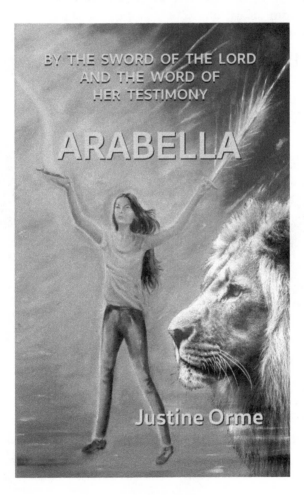

CPSIA information can be obtained
at www.ICGtesting.com
Printed in the USA
LVHW011210220322
714085LV00003B/473

9 780648 588351